Inclined Planes

by Michael Dahl

Bridgestone Books
an Imprint of Capstone Press

Bridgestone Books are published by Capstone Press
818 North Willow Street, Mankato, Minnesota 56001
Copyright © 1996 by Capstone Press
Printed in the United States of America

Library of Congress Cataloging-in-Publication Data
Dahl, Michael S.
    Inclinded planes/by Michael S. Dahl
    p. cm. -- (Early reader science. Simple machines)
    Includes bibliographical references and index.
    Summary: Describes many different kinds, uses, and benefits of inclined planes.
    ISBN 1-56065-447-3
    1. Simple machines--Juvenile literature. 2. Inclined planes--Juvenile literature. [1. Inclined
planes.] I. Title. II. Series
TJ147.D32 1996
621.8'11--dc20

                    96-27768
                    CIP
                      AC

Photo credits
FPG, 12, 18; James Levin, 6. International Stock, 16; Randy Masser, 14.
Chuck Place: 20. Stokka Productions, cover. Visuals Unlimited/Mark E.
Gibson, 8; Jeff Greenberg, 4; John Sohlden, 10.

Table of Contents

Words in **boldface** type in the text are defined in the Words to Know section in the back of this book.

Machines

Machines are any **tools** that help people do work. An inclined plane is a machine. A water slide is an example of an inclined plane.

What Is a Plane?

A plane is any flat surface. A sheet of paper, a table top, a floor, and a street are all planes. The cover of a book is a plane, too.

Inclined Planes

An inclined plane is any plane that has one end higher than the other. A playground slide is an inclined plane. Using an inclined plane, you can move from a high place to a low place or from a low place to a high place.

Make Work Easier

Inclined planes help people move heavy objects from one **height** to another. Post office workers use inclined planes to move packages from floor to floor. Trucks are often loaded and unloaded with inclined planes.

Move Things Faster

Inclined planes move things quickly. Most roofs on houses are inclined planes. When it rains, water falls from clouds in the sky. Inclined-plane roofs keep water from **pooling** and leaking into the houses.

Steps and Ladders

An inclined plane does not have to be smooth. A stairway is an inclined plane. A ladder is an inclined plane. They are not smooth. But they are still tools that move people and things up and down.

Ramps

A person in a wheelchair cannot climb stairs or a ladder. A wheelchair can move easily up a smooth ramp, though. The ramp is an inclined plane.

Ramps That Curve

Cars, trucks, and motorcycles use inclined planes every time they take a ramp on or off a highway. Most highway ramps curve around like a circle. Highway ramps are inclined planes that bring vehicles from one level to another.

The Wedge

A doorstop is a special kind of inclined plane called a **wedge**. A heavy door will stop when it runs into a powerful little inclined plane. Like other inclined planes, wedges make our work easier.

Hands On: Test the Power of Inclined Planes

Inclined planes give us an **advantage** when moving heavy objects. This experiment will show you if it is easier to use a long inclined plane or a short one.

What You Need
- Two boards, one short and one long
- A shoe box
- A can of soup
- A short piece of string
- A thick rubber band

What You Do

1. Tie one end of the string around the soup can. Tie the other end around the rubber band.
2. Place one end of the short board on the box and the other end on the floor.
3. Drag the soup can up the inclined plane by pulling on the rubber band. Notice how long the rubber band stretches.
4. Put the longer board up on the shoe box.
5. Drag the can up the second, longer inclined plane. Notice that the rubber band stretches less than before.

It takes less effort to move objects up the longer inclined plane. But it takes more time. The shorter slope requires more effort and less time.

Words to Know

advantage—an extra gain that makes something easier to do

height—the distance something is above a surface such as the ground

pooling—when liquids collect and make a puddle

tool—anything a person uses to get a job done

wedge—a special kind of inclined plane with a sharp edge at its low end

Read More

Ardley, Neil. *The Science Book of Machines*. New York:
Harcourt Brace Jovanovich, 1992.

Baker, Wendy. *Machines*. New York: Thomson Learning, 1994.

Lampton, Christopher. *Bathtubs, Slides, Roller Coaster Rails*.
Brookfield, Conn.: The Millbrook Press, 1991.

Ward, Alan. *Machines At Work*. Chicago: Franklin Watts, 1993.

Index